Battered, Bruised, but Never Broken

AF624561

Madison Lesher

BookLeaf Publishing

Battered, Bruised, but Never Broken © 2021
Madison Lesher

All rights reserved.

No part of this publication may be reproduced, stored in a retrieval system, or transmitted, in any form or by any means, electronic, mechanical, photocopying, recording or otherwise, without the prior written permission of the presenters.

Madison Lesher asserts the moral right to be identified as author of this work.

Presentation by *BookLeaf Publishing*

Web: www.bookleafpub.com

E-mail: info@bookleafpub.com

ISBN - 9789357445252

First edition 2021

DEDICATION

For the women who ever felt these emotions or lived in these situations. Scream it for the world to hear, scream loud and break their eardrums.

For my family, we've been through it these past couple years and I just wanted to say that I love you all. I may not show it or say it often, but I do. I love you, no matter what.

ACKNOWLEDGEMENT

I'd like to thank BookLeaf Publishing for this opportunity. I never imagined that I would publish my own work before and, through you, you made it happen, a true dream come true.

Thank you to my dad, for getting me started on my reading path. Without you, who knows what my tastes would've been like.

Thank you, mom, for giving me the idea of what I want to do with my life.

Thank you to Ashley, my bestie, who is always editing and offering suggestions on my work. I know I can pest you sometimes, but I really appreciate it!

Finally, thank you Pappy. Who knew what started out as a joke between us would turn into a genuine interest?

Once Upon a Time

That's how
it always
begins.

A King,
A prince,
saves
the princess,
the damsel.

But what happens
when
the saviors
are the
villains
in disguise?

Does she
crumble?
Is she
too shattered?

Or
does she
break free?
And slay
the dragons.

what love is I

As children
we think
the world is perfect.

As children
we see
our parents happy.

As children,
we have
rose colored lenses
over our eyes.

As children,
we see what they
want us to see.

And that family
is nothing less
than perfect.

do you think about it too?

We were close once
but I couldn't do it
anymore.

I just wanted
to know
your thoughts.

But you snapped
and I cracked.

Now
there's a chasm
where our
bond
used to be.

we're getting a divorce
I

Did you know?
That it was
one week
before my
birthday
when you
announced…

Happy Birthday
    to you

"…we're getting a divorce."

Do you realize?

Do you realize
that you
tell me
things
that I
don't really
want to know?

Get it off
your chest,
do not
hold it
inside.
That is
good advice.

Except now
it is on
my shoulders.
Except now
I must hold it
inside.

So,
I ask you,
what do
I do with

these secrets,
these truths
that can,
that will,
that do
make everything
worse?

Do you realize
I'm not
your therapist?

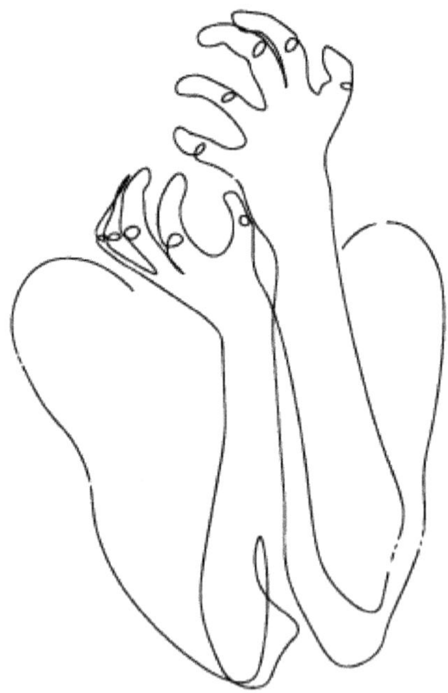

what love is II

What heals, yet hurts?

What can be given, yet taken?

What provides warmth when you have it,
but leaves you cold when it's gone?

Love.

Children no longer,
the rosy lenses are smudged.

We realize love is not so simple.
In fact,
it may be
the most
complicated emotion.

It is irrational
to try and
define such an
emotion.

So how do
you think
you can
define me?

what i can't say

It's in your head.
~~but it's not~~

You're imagining things.
~~but i'm not~~

You're lucky I'm even
interested in you.
~~am i?~~

Why must you make me do this?
~~i'd give anything to make you stop~~

I just love you so much!
~~is that what the bruises mean?~~

No one would believe you.
~~maybe you're right.~~

a legitimate question

How many
times can
you
b
r
e
a
k
yourself
a p a r t
before
there is
nothing
left?

a legitimate answer

Break yourself
into smaller

and smaller,

and smaller

pieces
until there
is just
nothing left.

It's the same as
spreading yourself
too thin,
or
giving yourself
away.
Until there
is just
nothing
left.

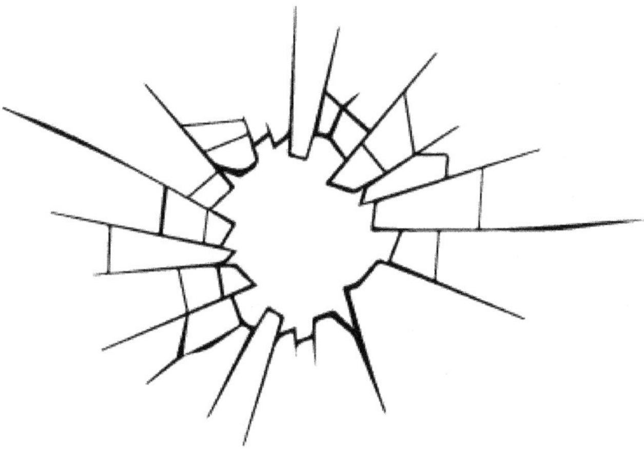

the mind they will never understand

They do not hear you.
They do not see you.
They will not ever.
You will not let them,
Hear you,
See you.

You won't show it,
But you're sinking
Down,
Down,
Always *down*, always further, and deeper.

Your mind is quicksand.
Your thoughts are grains of sand.
The more you try, the quicker you sink.
There is no way out, no way up,
Because imagination knows no bounds.

The sand closes over,
Over your head, over your mind.
And you drown.
In sand, in thoughts,
In worries and fear and
Anxiety.

You're tired,
Oh so tired,
So, you sleep, just to turn off
The thoughts, the worries,
And fears and anxieties.

But when you wake,
It all begins again.
Day after day, night after night.
Rinse and repeat, rinse and repeat.

But they will not see you.
They cannot see you.
Because you won't let them.

You smile and laugh,
Joke and Jest.
A voice is nagging,
That it's false,
A façade.
You continue to sink,
There is no bottom.
Because this is not a well,
Nor a gaping pit, or even the Mariana Trench.

It is your mind, your thoughts,
Your imagination.
And imagination knows no bounds.

This is your mentality, your way of life.
One riddled with anxiety.

Inescapable, unfathomable.

And so, you continue to fret.
You continue to fear.
Until you finally fall asleep,
Then it all disappears.

And when you wake,
It all
Begins
Again.
Day after day, night after night.
Rinse and repeat.

If I kill myself for you, is it murder?

An endless ocean of emotion,
Wave after wave of hurt.

I love you.

I cannot breathe
Under the waves
That are pummeling me.

Lacking oxygen.
Brain flooded.
Mind shutting down.

I love you.

Just one more chance,
You beg me.

I give in, just once more.

Hope is a shore that I will never see.
For you use up the chance.
You use up the air.

The cycle does not end, it never does.

Not until I wear myself to the bone,
Push the body and mind ‘til they break.
And then some.

I love you.

I must keep swimming, keep moving,
Or I’ll drown in the feeling
of my (broken) heart
b r e a k i n g.

So, I tell myself:
Just. One. More.

None of it matters though,
not for all the effort
I could ever muster.
For, I am not drown*ing*.

I am drown*ed*.

In the endless sea,
of you
and just one more

I love you.

an epiphany

I never expected
for it to end
this way.

We were fine,
or were we?

Belladonna kisses,
Words coated in arsenic.

Slow, undetectable.
We were dying, dying,
dead.

What I didn’t realize
was that it was you.

It was your words
that leached
the warmth.

Your actions
that bled
me dry.

Until there was nothing
but a corpse.

Cold, still, dead.

And it was then
that I realized
sometimes
the person
you'd take
the bullet for
is behind
the gun.

we're getting a divorce
II

Sometimes
the best thing
is to let go.

It hurts
worse than
anything.
But it
is necessary.

Let go.

You deserve
to be happy.
You deserve
more.

And so,
they break.
 s p l i t
Are no more.

They let go.

what love is III

Love can bloom
when properly
cared for.

Love can wilter
under the toxic
circumstances.

Love is a flower,
delicate, sensitive.

Love is powerful,
and in the wrong hands,
it can mean
the difference
between
living for you
or living
for them.

So you must decide
if you will let it
die
or let it
grow.

a new life, just not *your* new life

Being single
means freedom.

You just can't
sleep around,
be your
own person,
color outside
the cookie cutter
mold
that man
built.

You are a woman.
You
have children.
You
cook.
You
clean.
You
stay silent.

You will be thin,
but not

unhealthily thin.
You will be pretty,
but not
unnaturally pretty.

If you refuse,
society condemns
your behavior,
your decisions,
your thoughts,
your opinions,
your dreams,
your newfound life.

You will obey,
and nothing else.
No more,
no less.
Society decrees
it so.

and so, we take back the narrative

You will judge me for my decisions.
It is inevitable really.
What I do with my life, my mind,
my body, my being.

So cut me with your words,
Cut me with your intentions,
Stab me, slice me, scar me.
But you will not break me.
You cannot break me.
Because I will not let you.
Because I do not give you that power.

This isn't how it is supposed to be.
I am human, a person, too,
we should be equal.
But all you see is female.
And this is how it is.

You only see worth in my gender.
But what you don't see is
I am me, and you will not take that away.
I am me, and you cannot take that away.
Because I do not give you that power.

My name is whatever I want it to be
I am whatever, whoever I chose to be.
I make my choices for me, not you.

So, you can take
your patriarchy
and burn
on the stakes
of the
witches
of old.

You can call me names
for not giving you what you want,
for not doing what you want.

I am the narrator of this story; you aren't even in it.
Not even to be
the villain.
You are power*less* and I am power*ful*.

I am me, and you don't scare me.

a different type of love

We become
so focused on
loving another,
we forget to
love ourselves.

We forget to
put ourselves first.

We forget to
prioritize our health,
emotionally and physically.

We forget
that we matter
just as much
as them.

aftermath

The dragons have awoken.
They are raging
to the sun.

How dare we
break free
from our towers
WiThOuT tHeM.

We break from
the pretty pink
princess plan

and become the
wicked witch
with withering
weapons.

fuck being the hero, be the villain

I am being
too sensitive.
I need
to grow
thicker skin.
Can't you take a joke?

No.

I am not here
to hold
your hand,
to stroke
your ego.

I am done
being a good girl,
a nice girl.

We've all got
blood
on our
hands.

I own mine.

You hide
yours
by blaming
me.

This is how
I become
the villain
to your
hero.

You ‘saved’ them
by burning
the witches
all those
years ago.
I ‘committed sin’
by not
conforming
to your
bullshit.

I am
the villain now

in man’s
history.

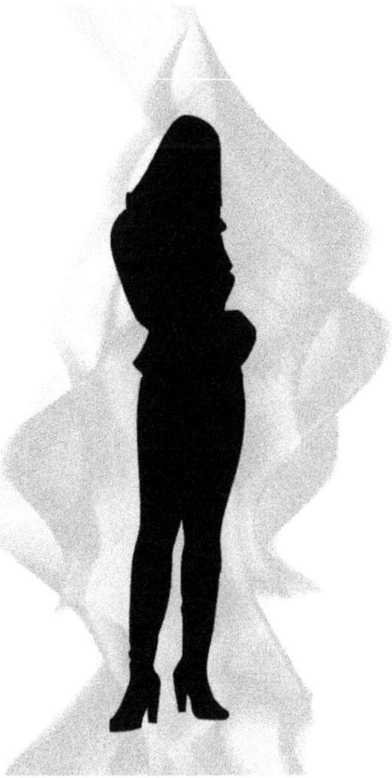

sugar and spice, and everything n(ice)

It is time.
Out with the old,
in with the new.

History called them witches,
men call us bitches.

You are all
wrong.
If you are
going to
write about
us
and our
evils.
At least get
our names right.

The shadow
behind the
throne
no longer.

Who are we?

We are
a motherfucking
G O D D E S S.

And Goddess trumps King.

The End

Once upon a time

That's how it
always began.

But when
the princes and kings
are the villains
in disguise,

But when
the saviors
batter
and bruise
those they
swore
to protect
and swore
to love,

something
e a r t h s h a t t e r i n g
and
w o r l d f o r m i n g

emerges
from the pieces

they left
behind.

And the women
who survived
to laugh and dance
over the
graves of men
lived happily
ever
after.

www.ingramcontent.com/pod-product-compliance
Lightning Source LLC
Chambersburg PA
CBHW051739130826
49812CB00033B/920
9789357445252